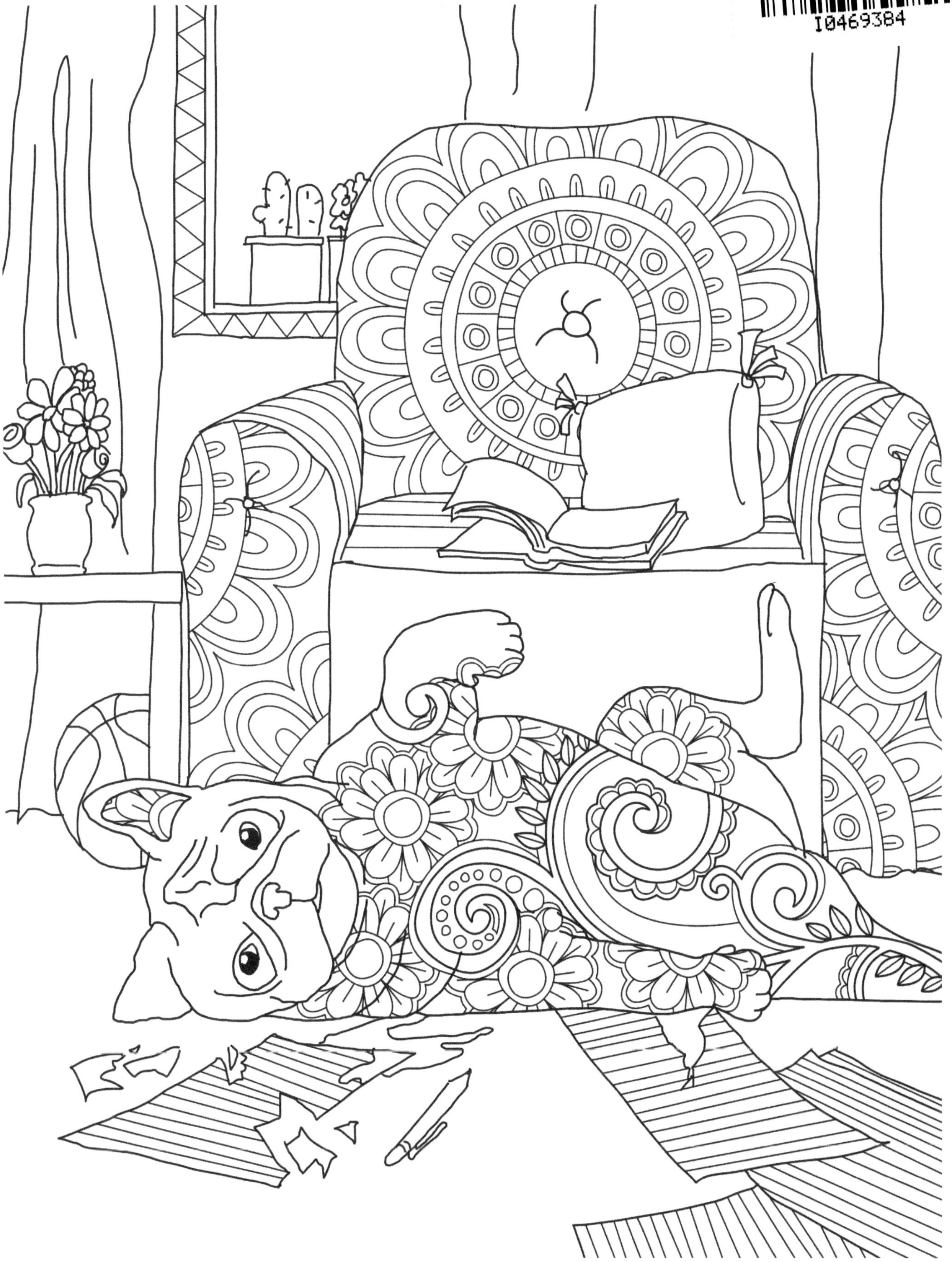

Illustrated by:
Mandala & Caricature Illustration
Joshua Lazana Lagman and Jade Villaremo

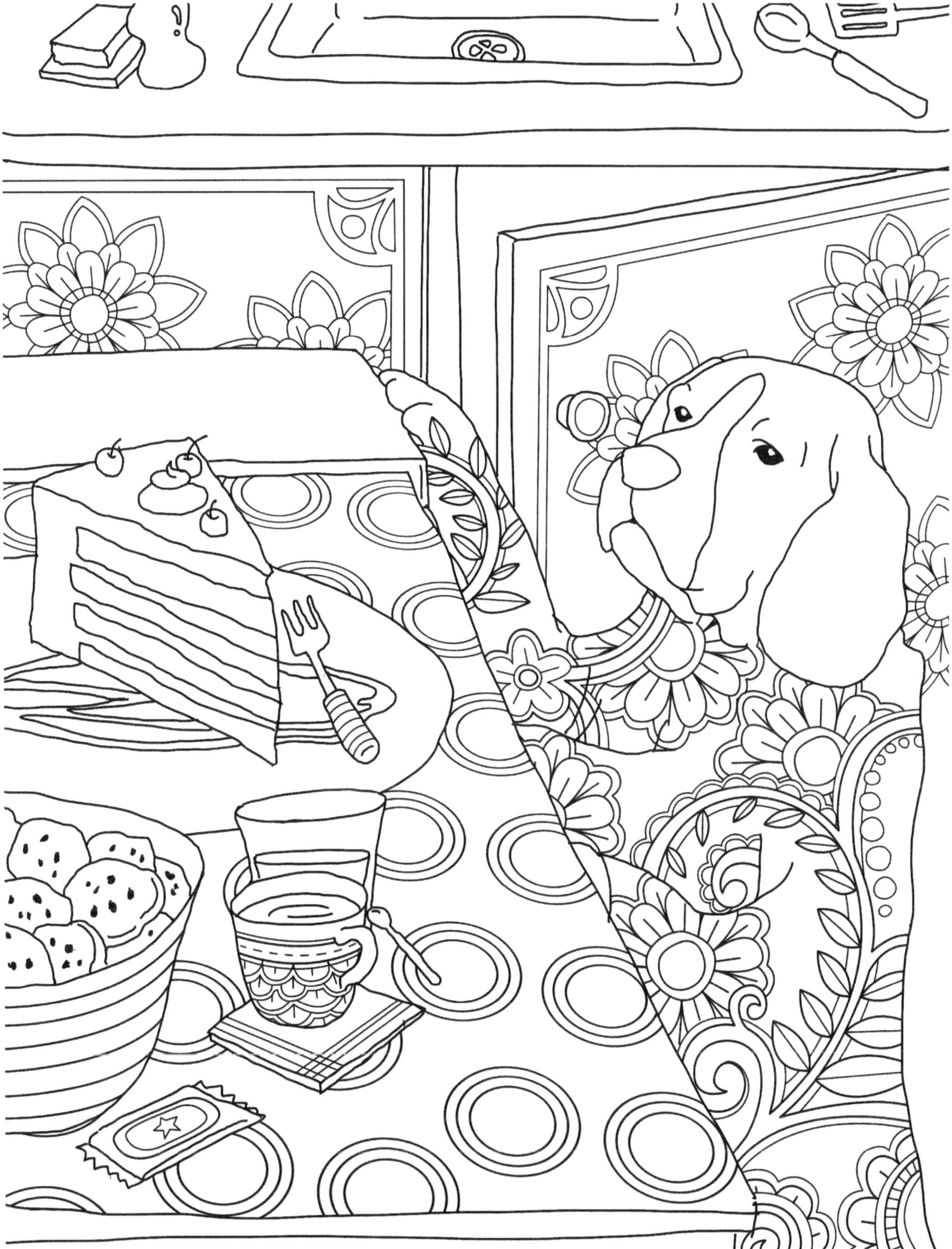

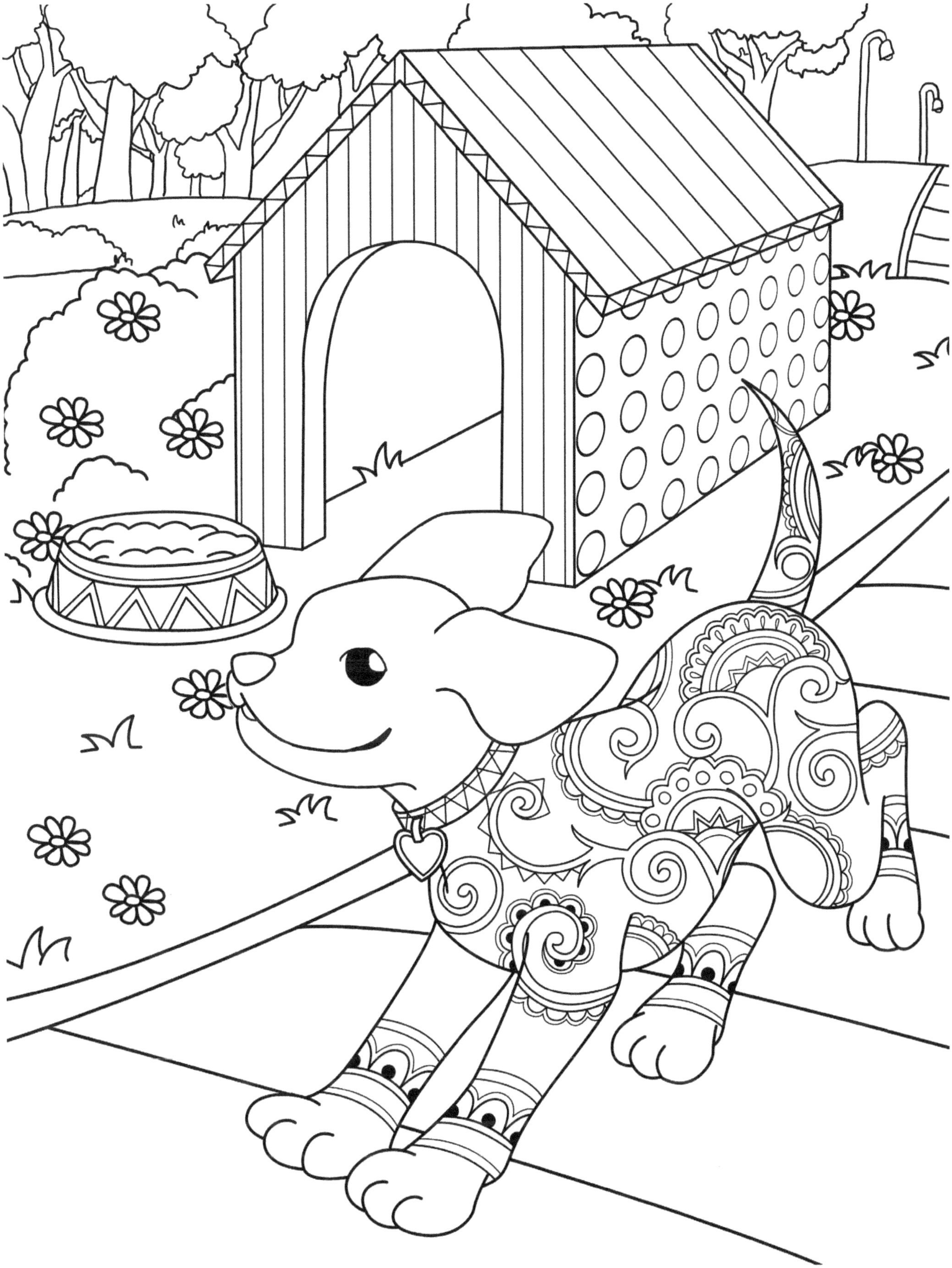

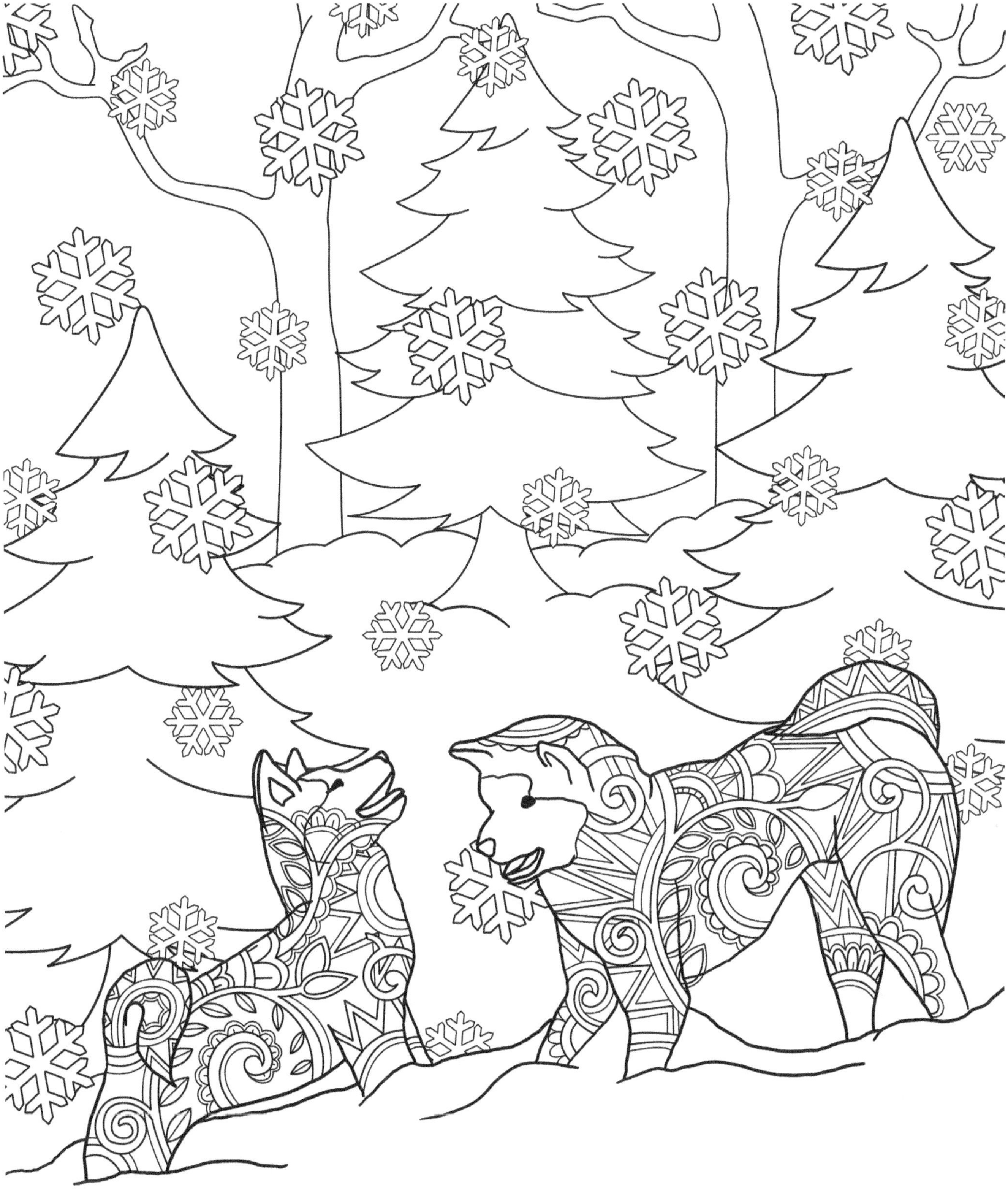

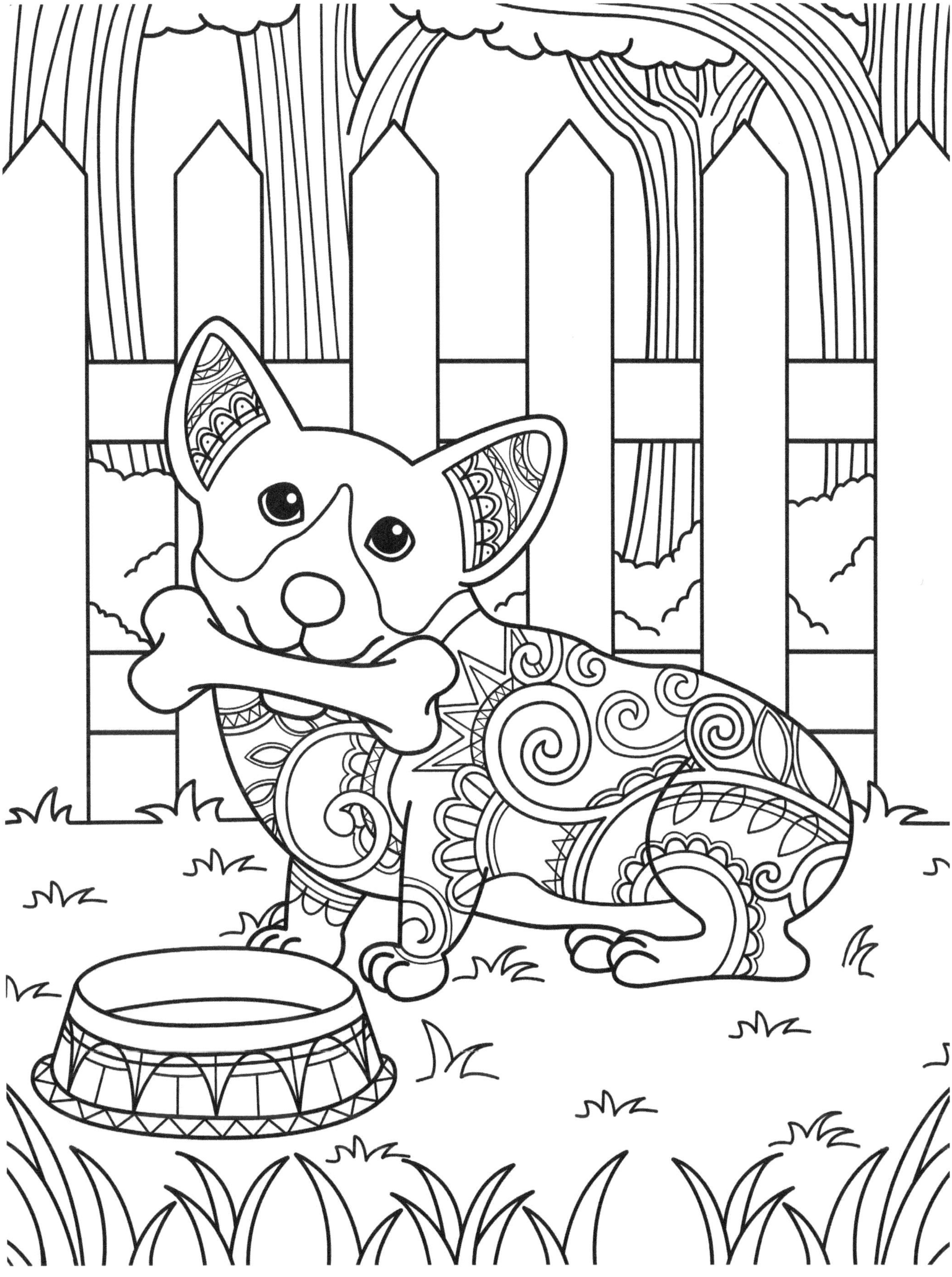

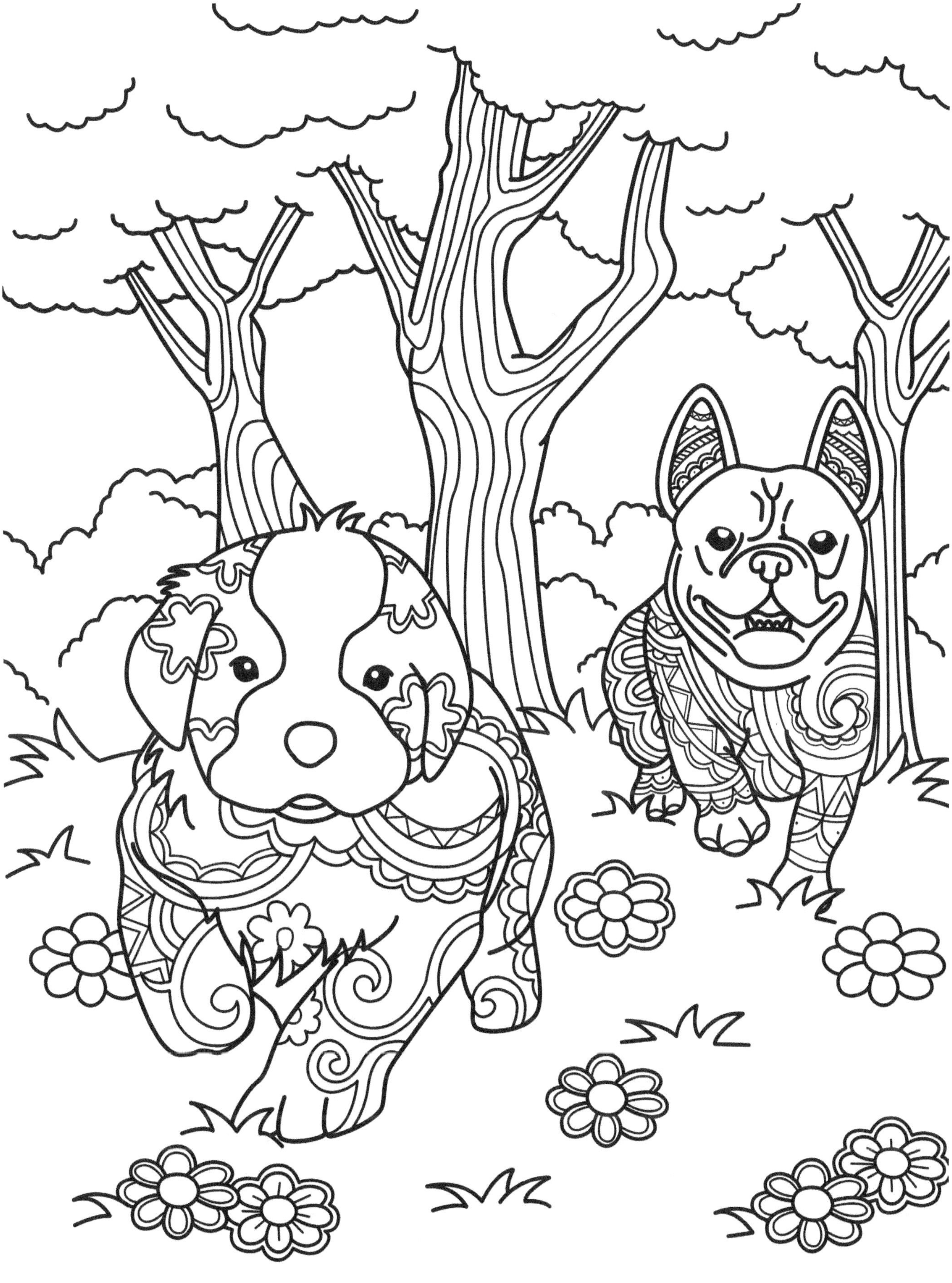

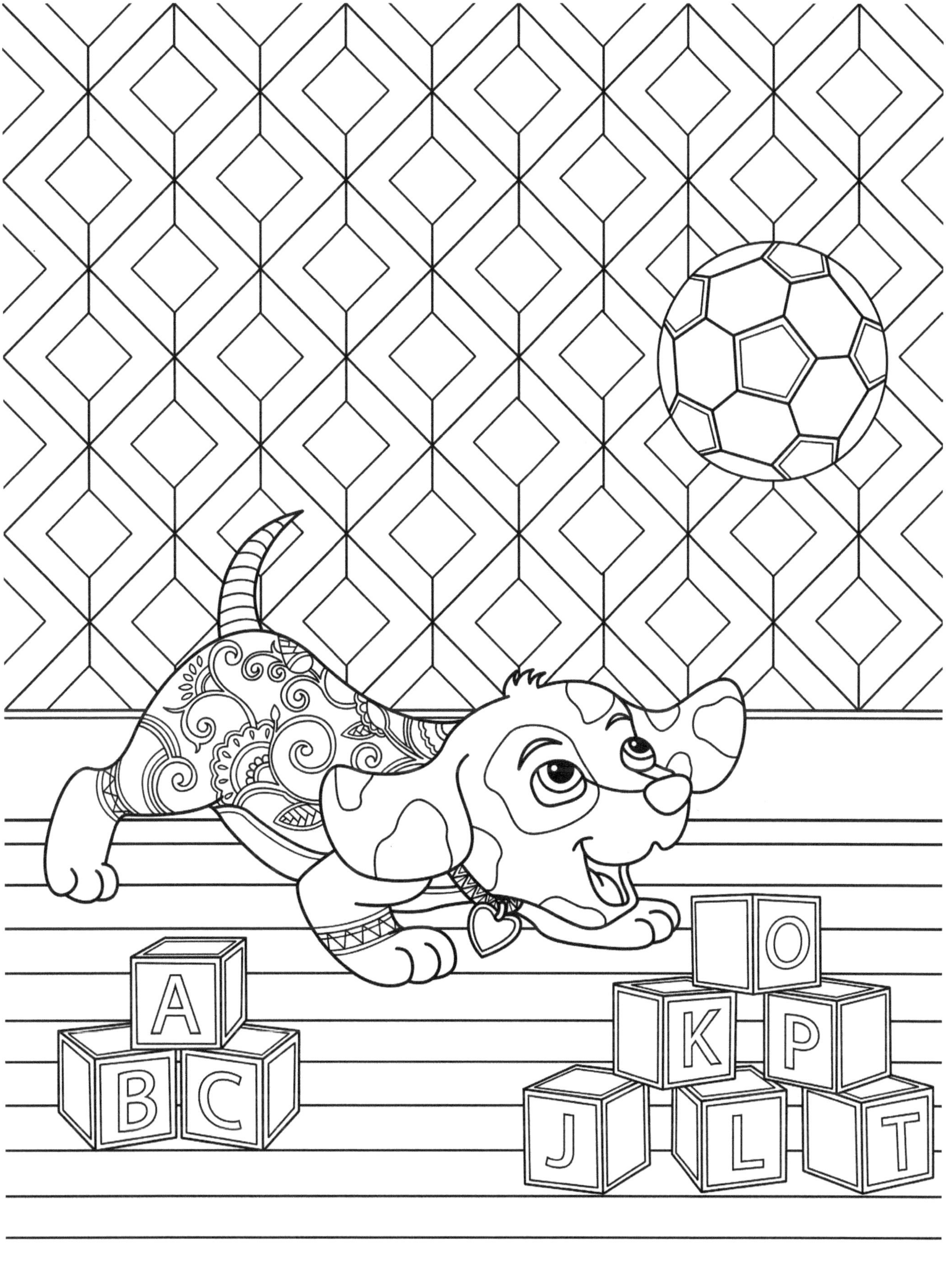
A
B
C
O
K
P
J
L
T

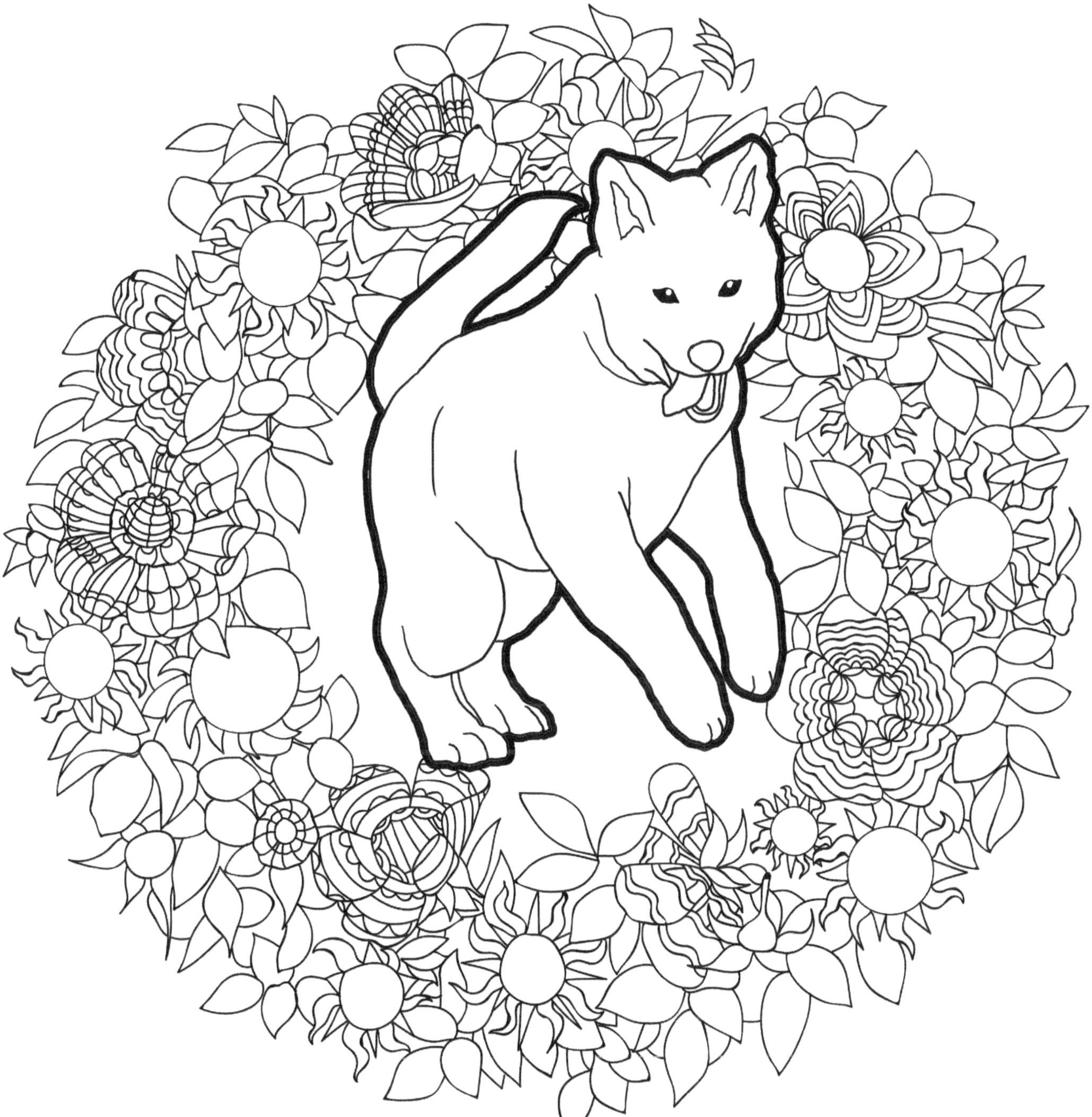

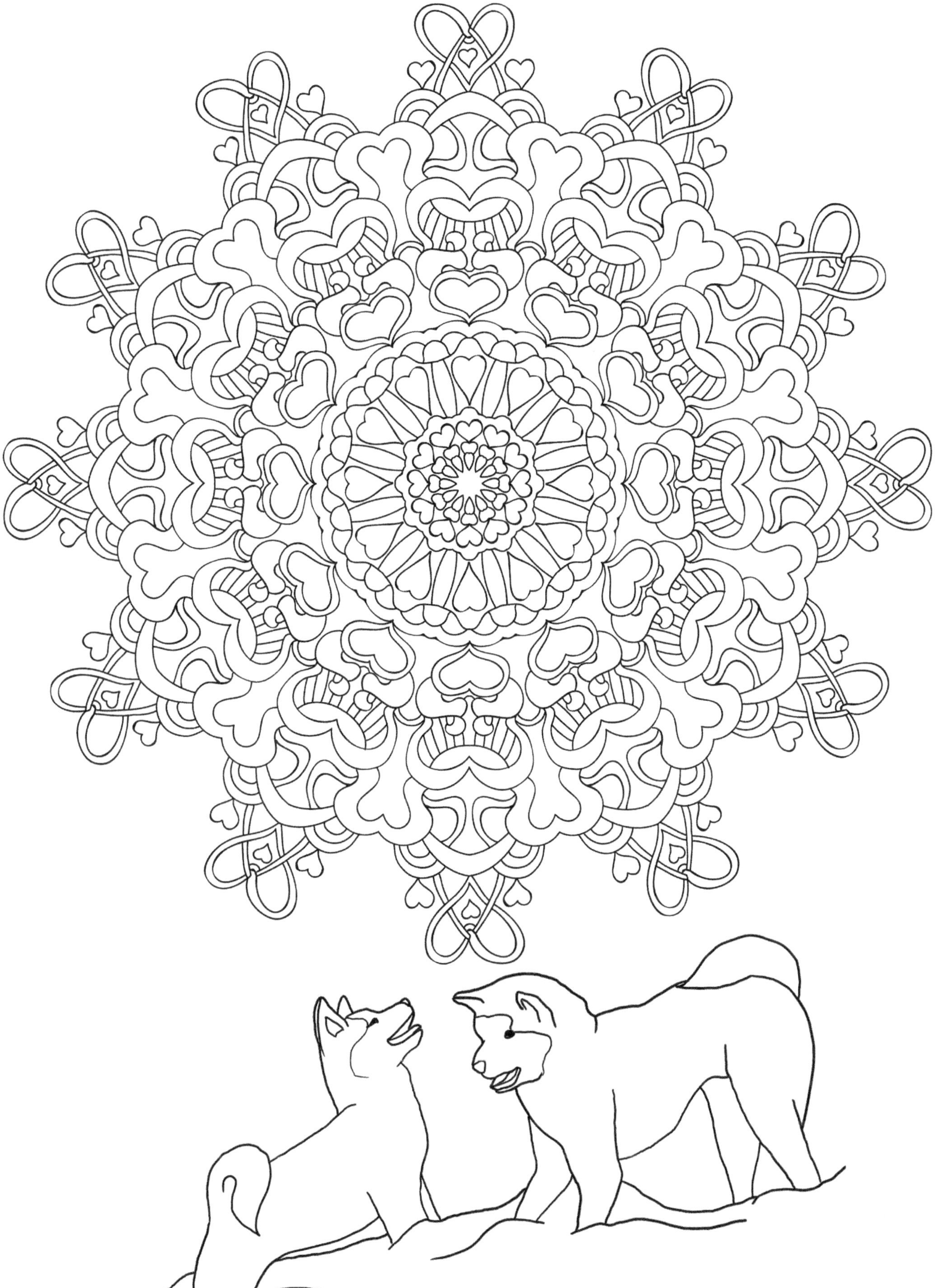

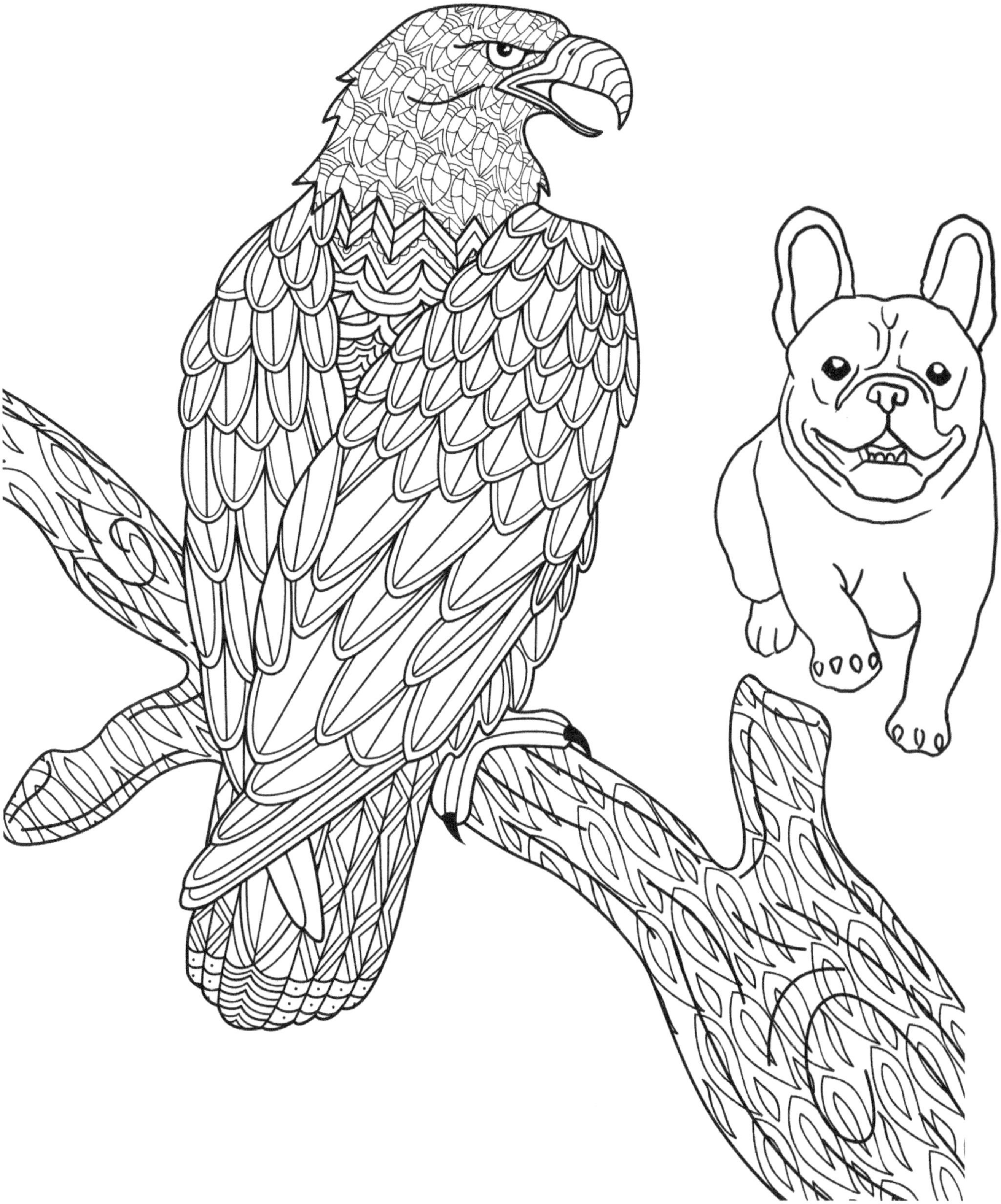

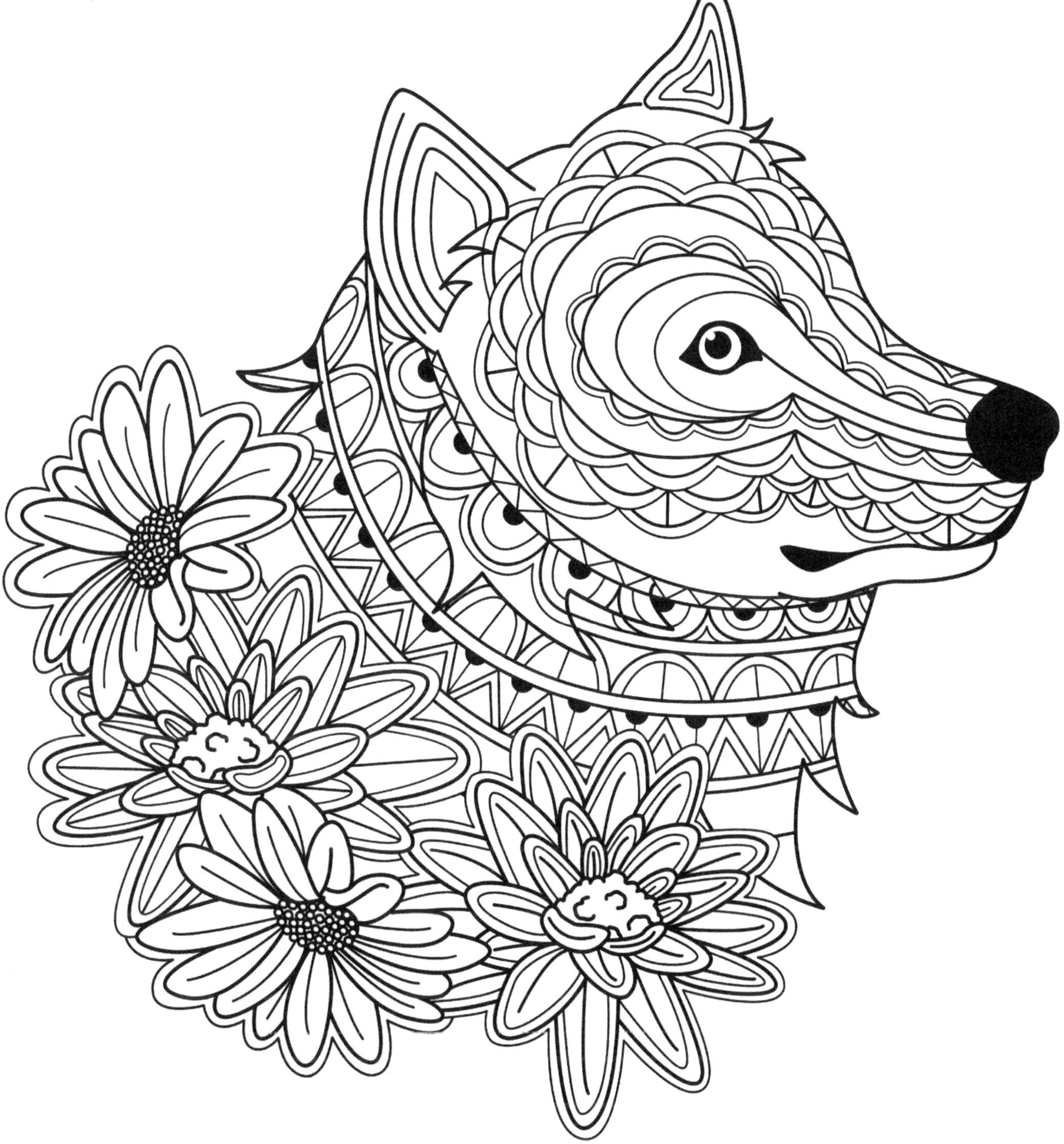

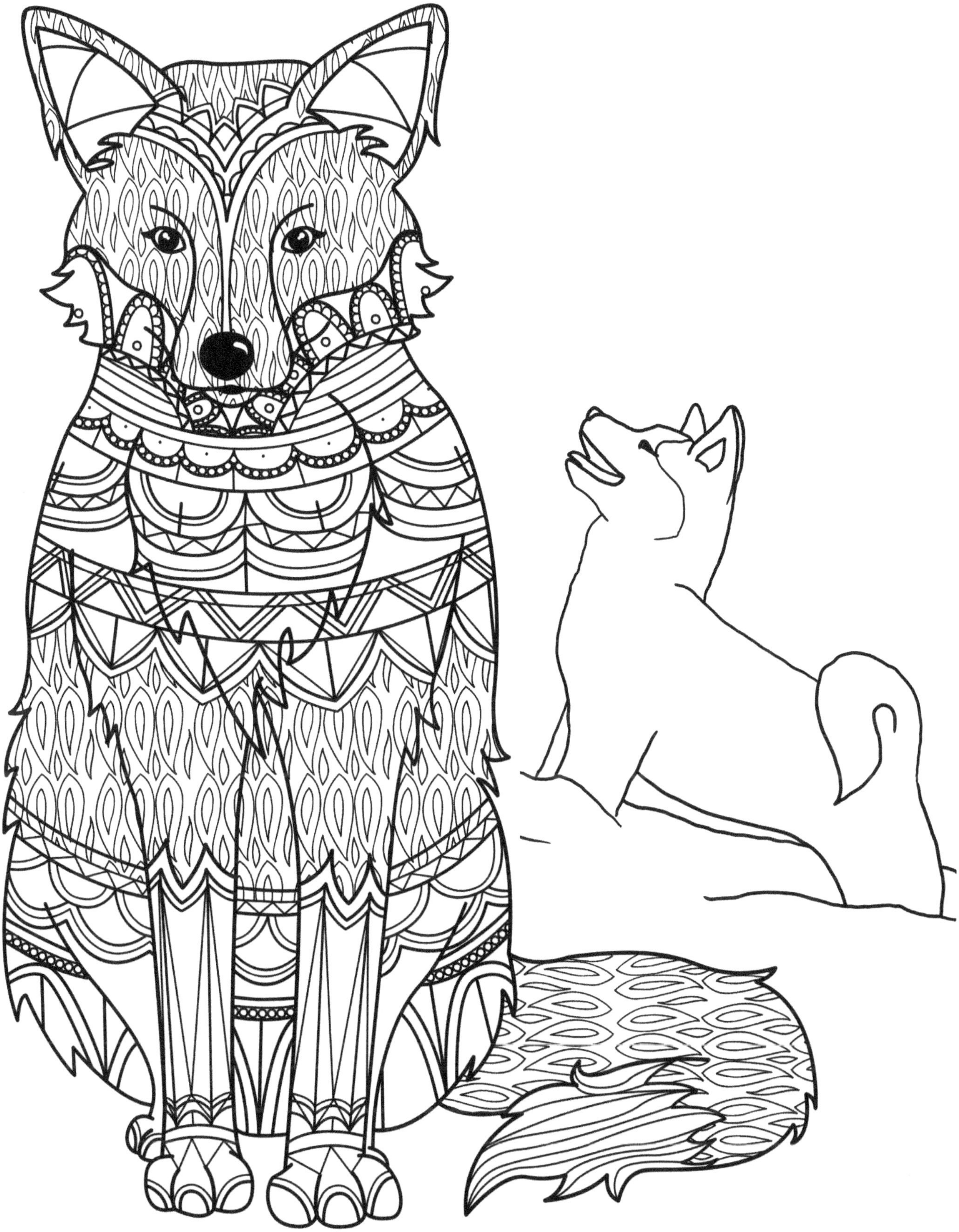

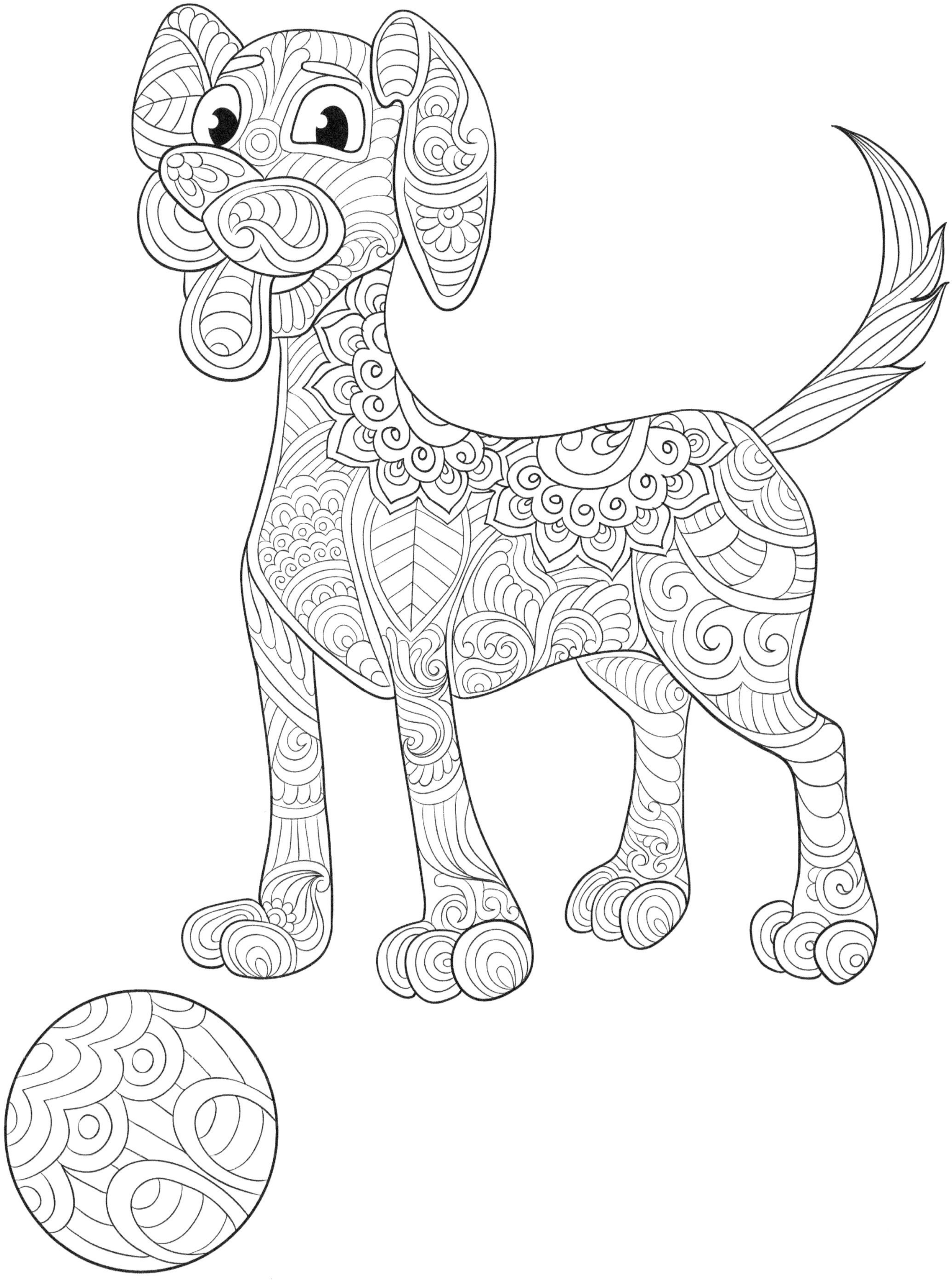

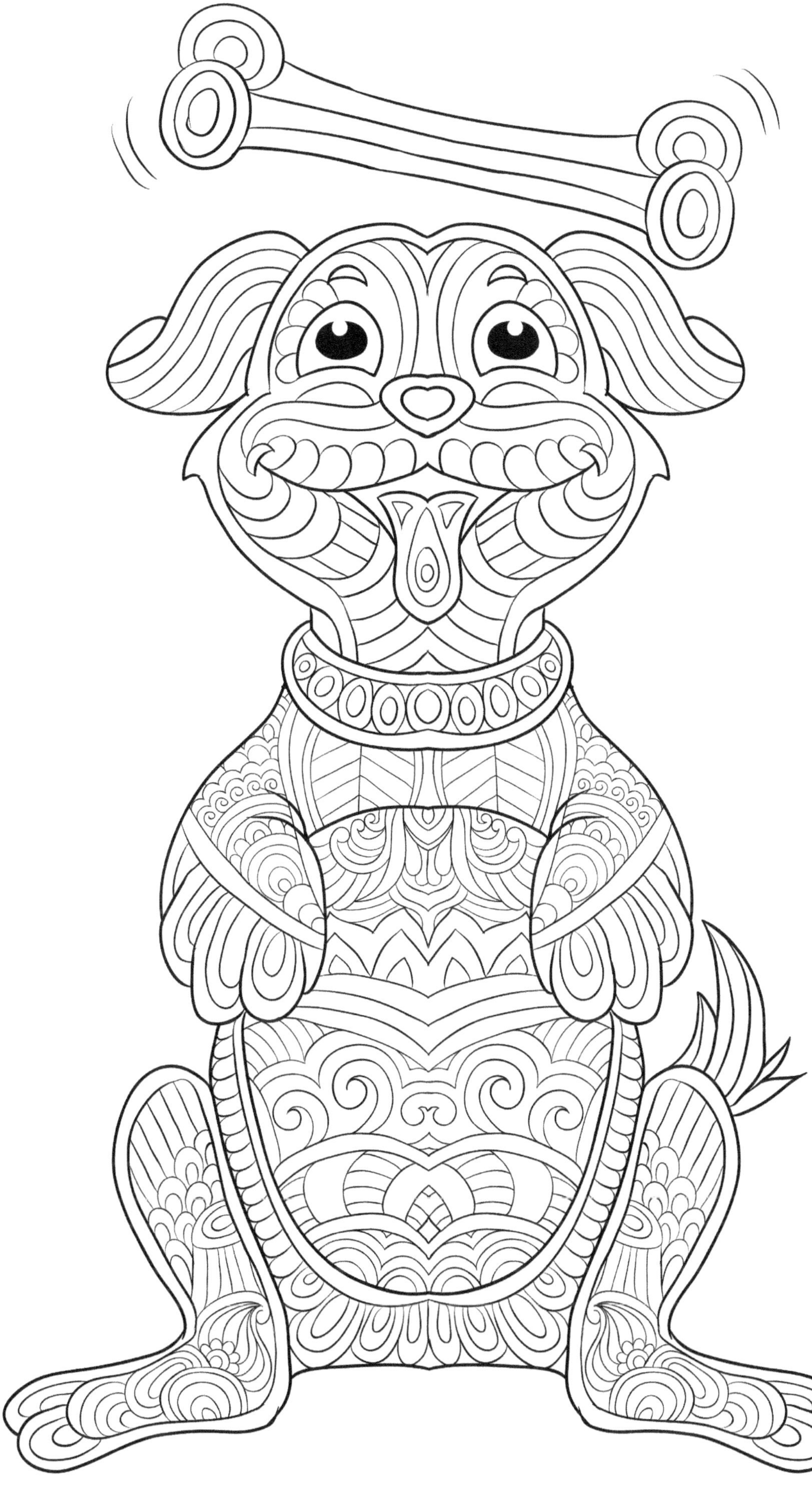

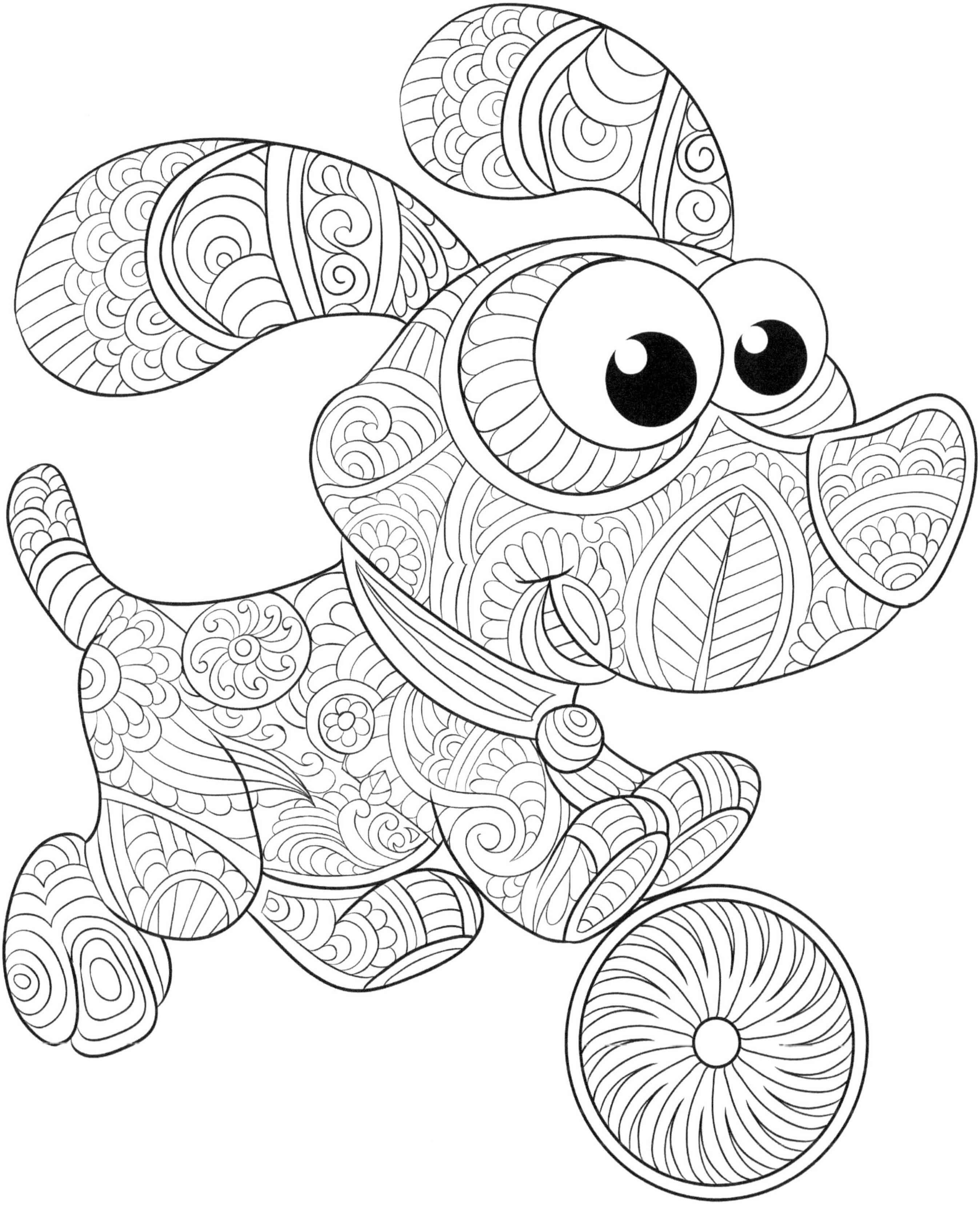

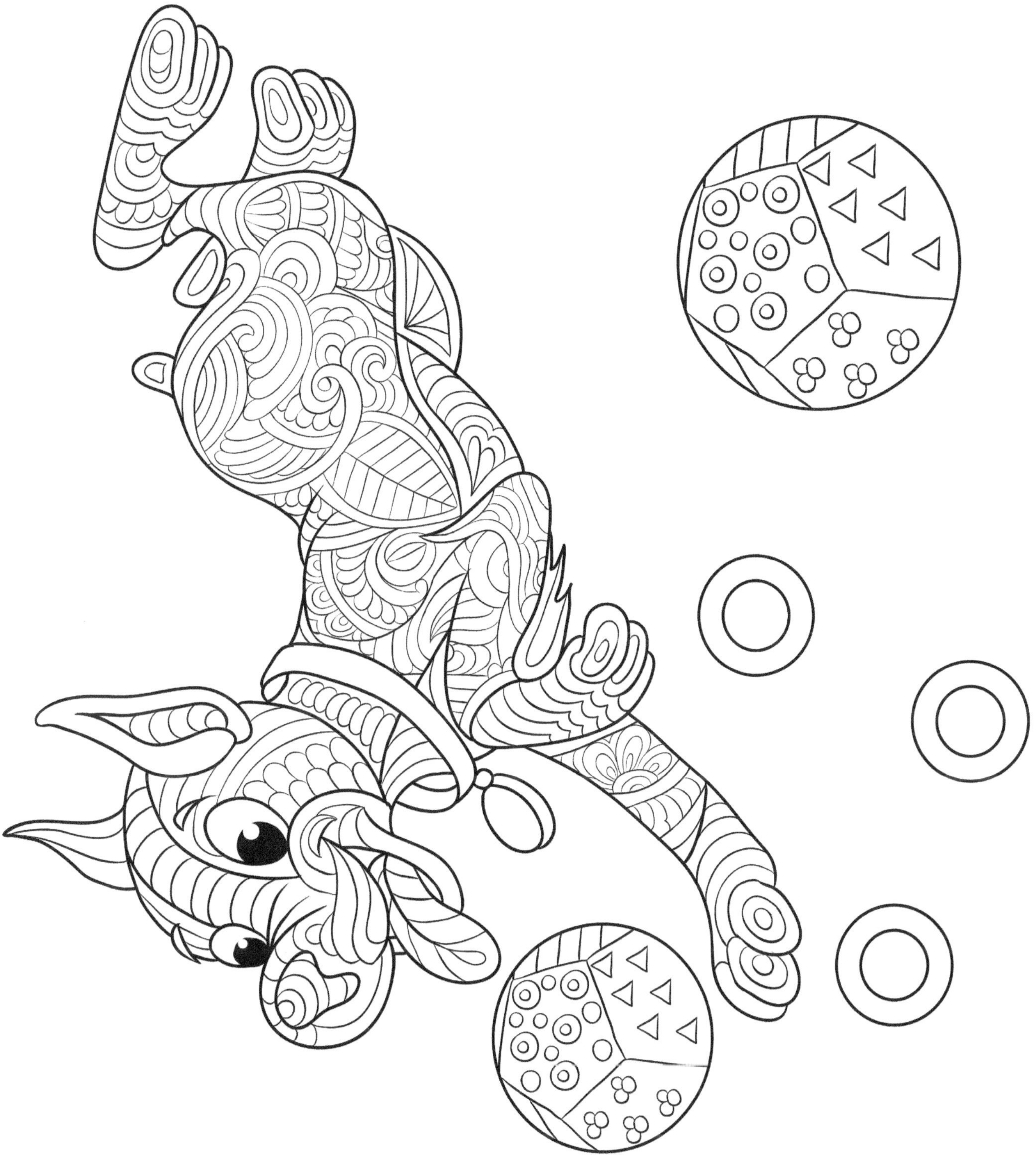

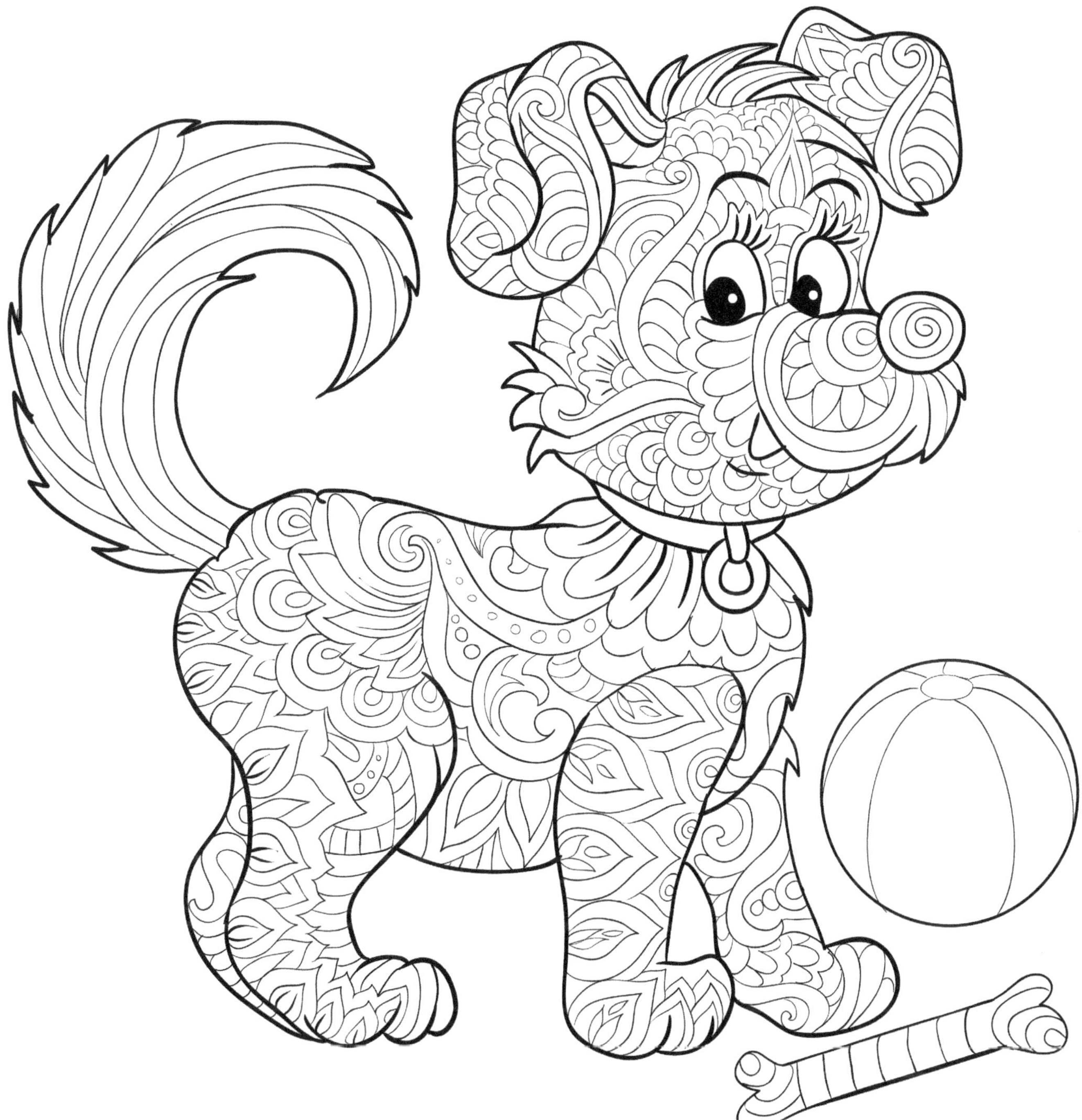

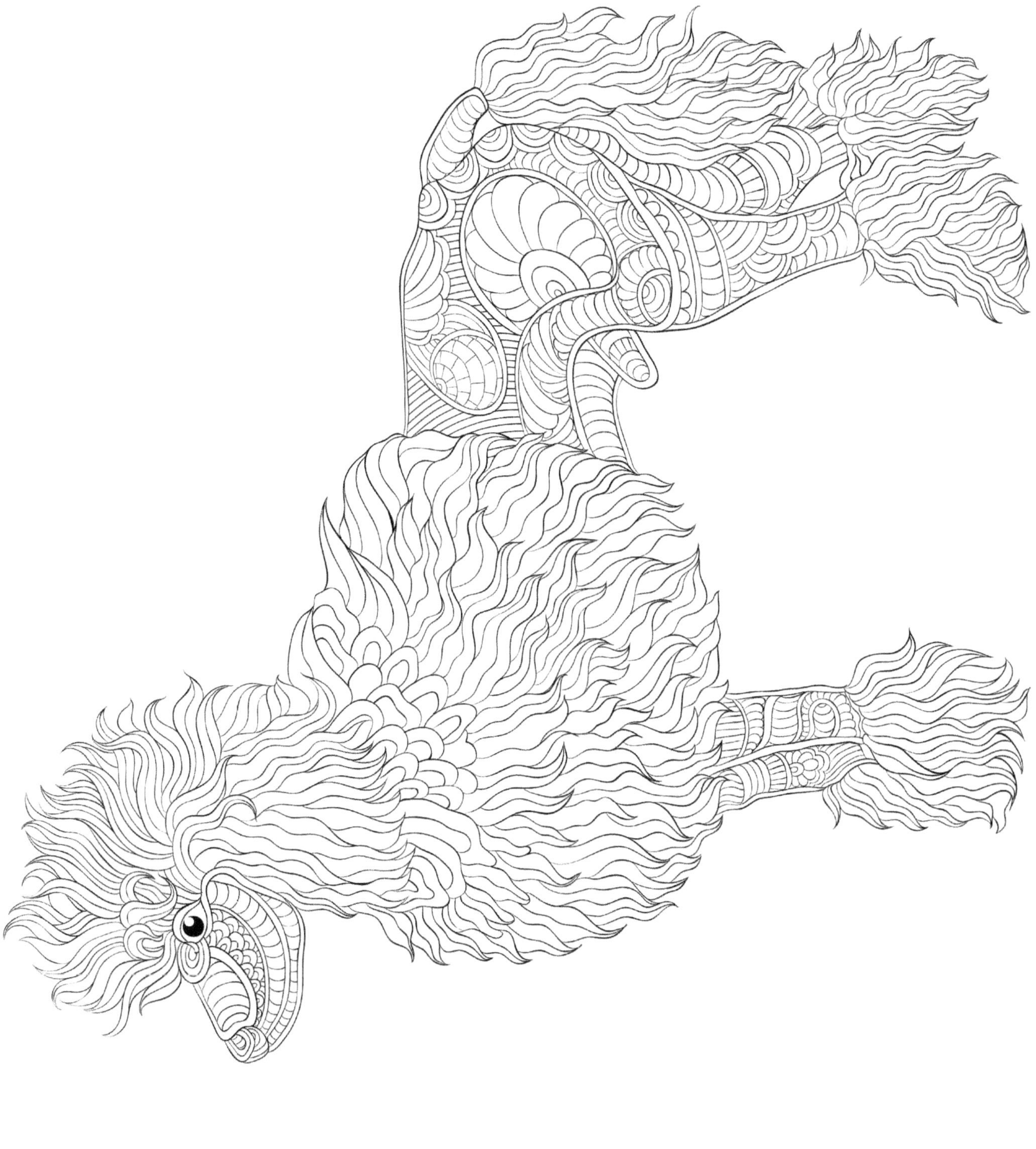

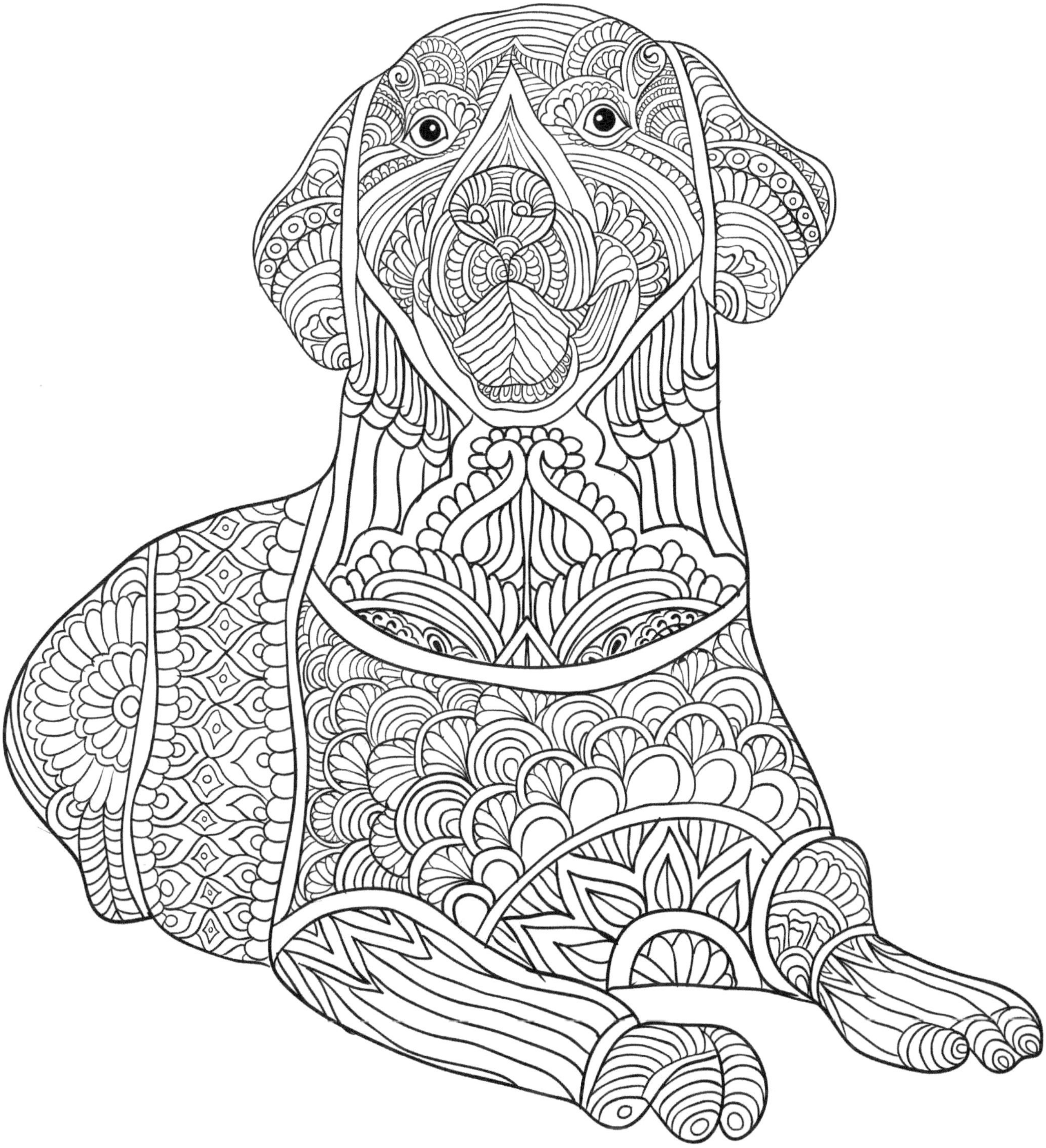

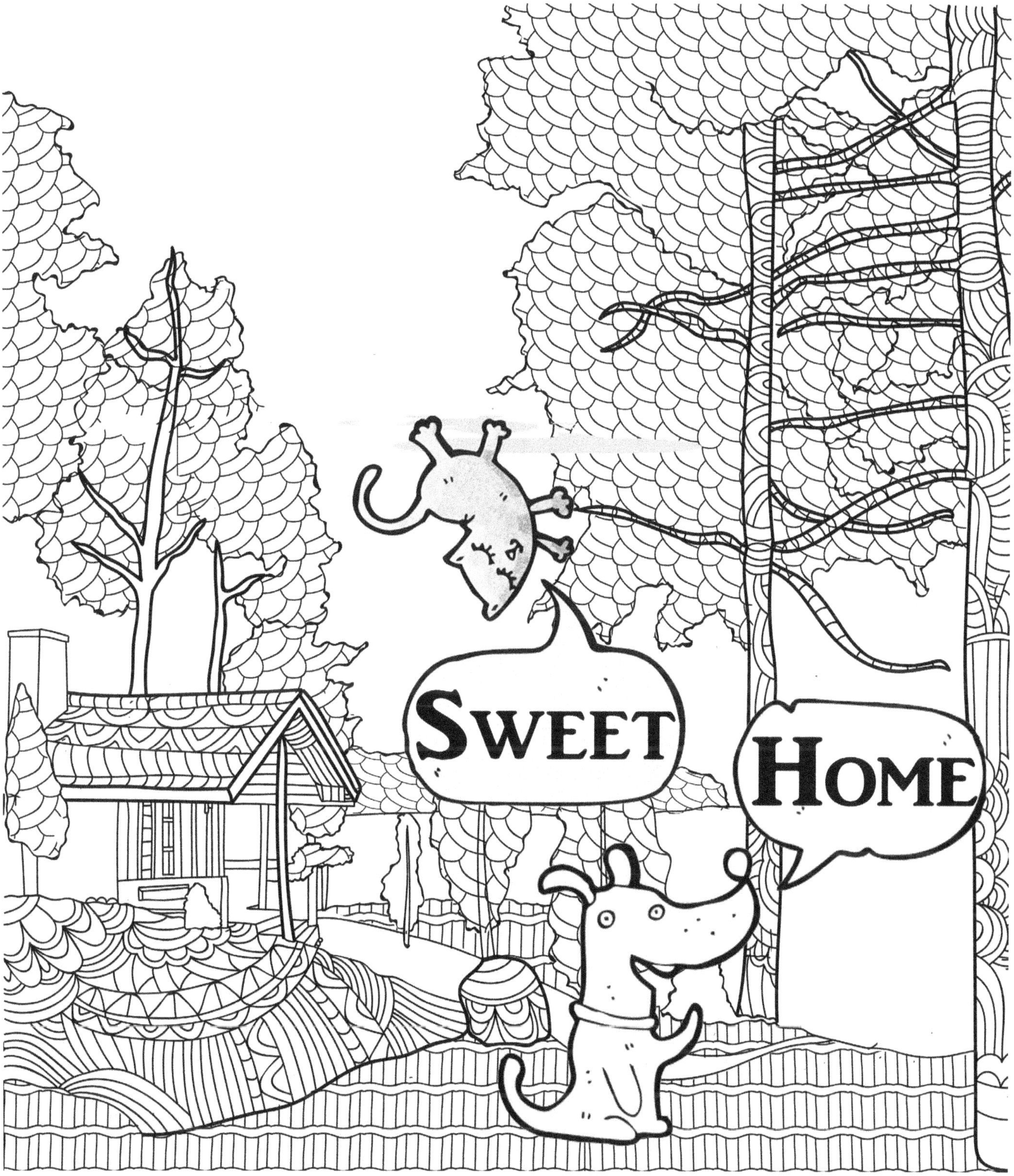
SWEET
HOME

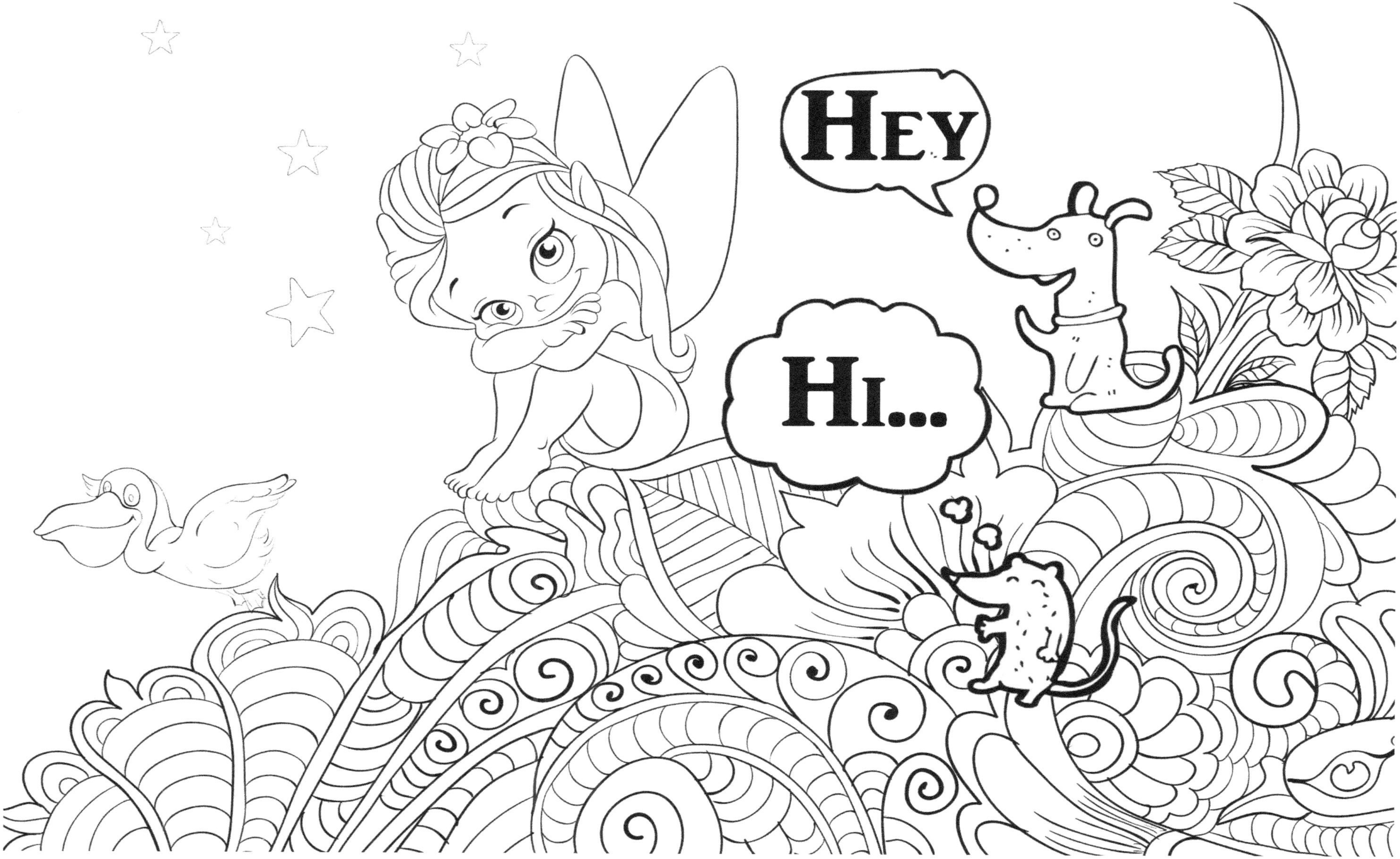
HEY
HI...

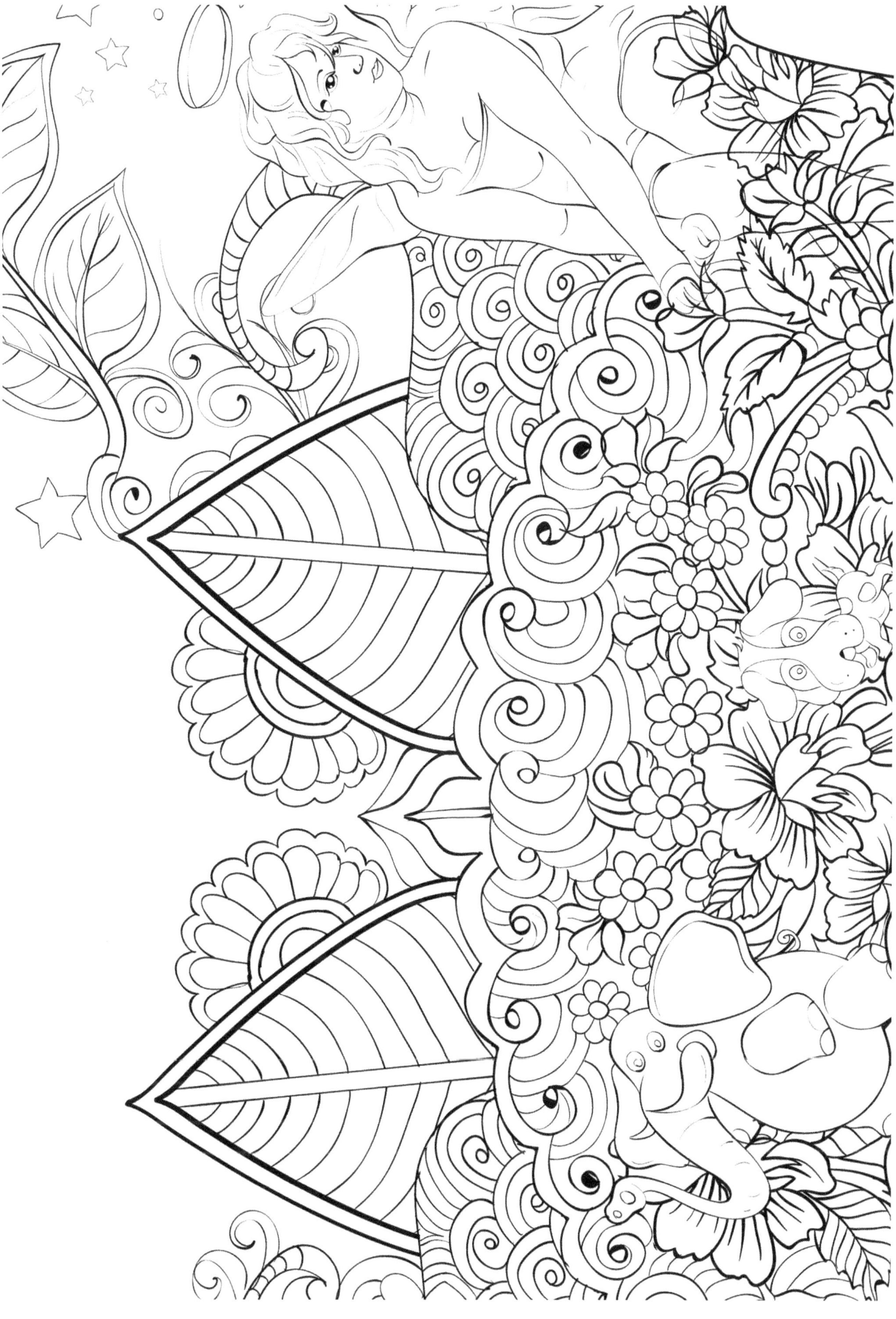

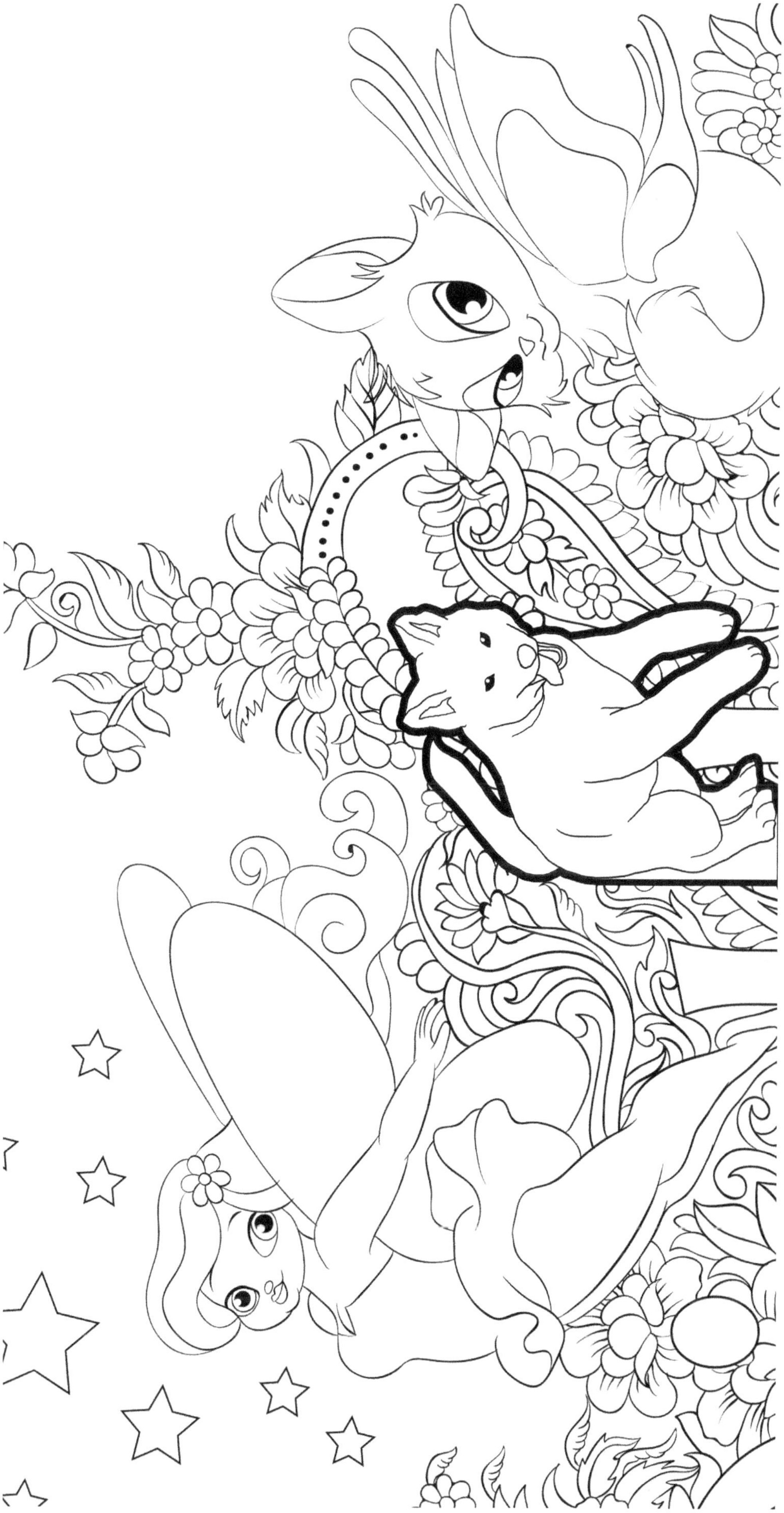

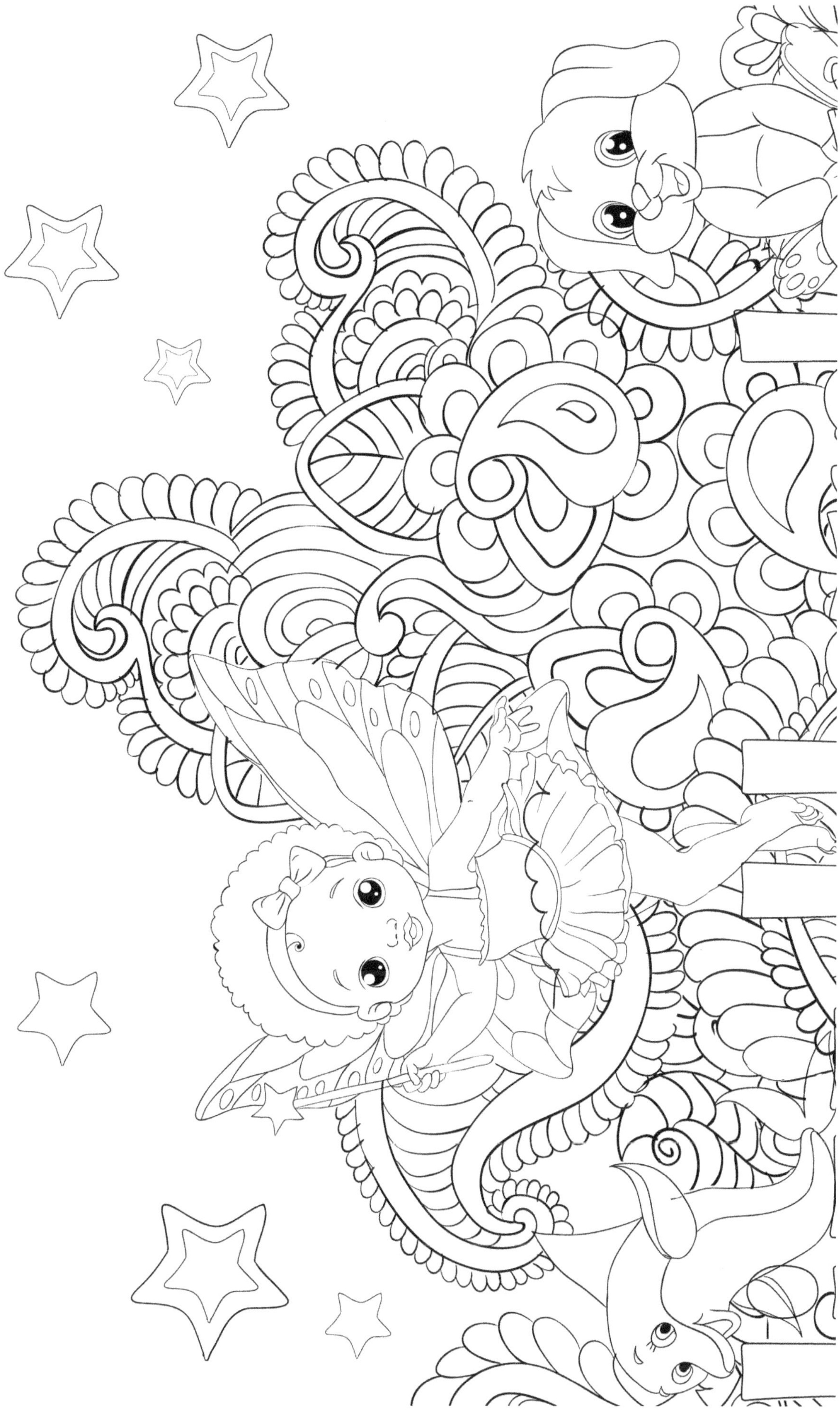

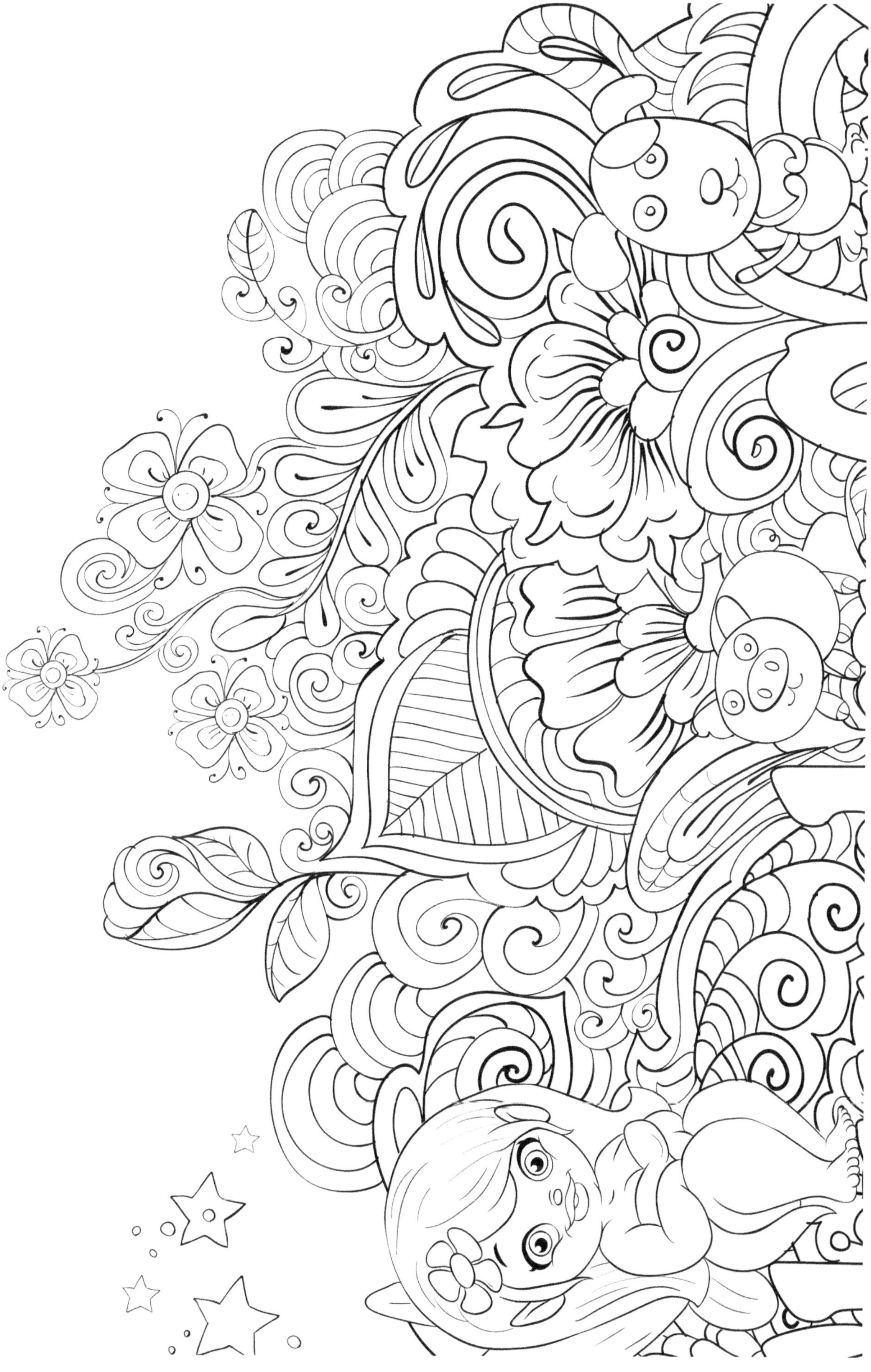

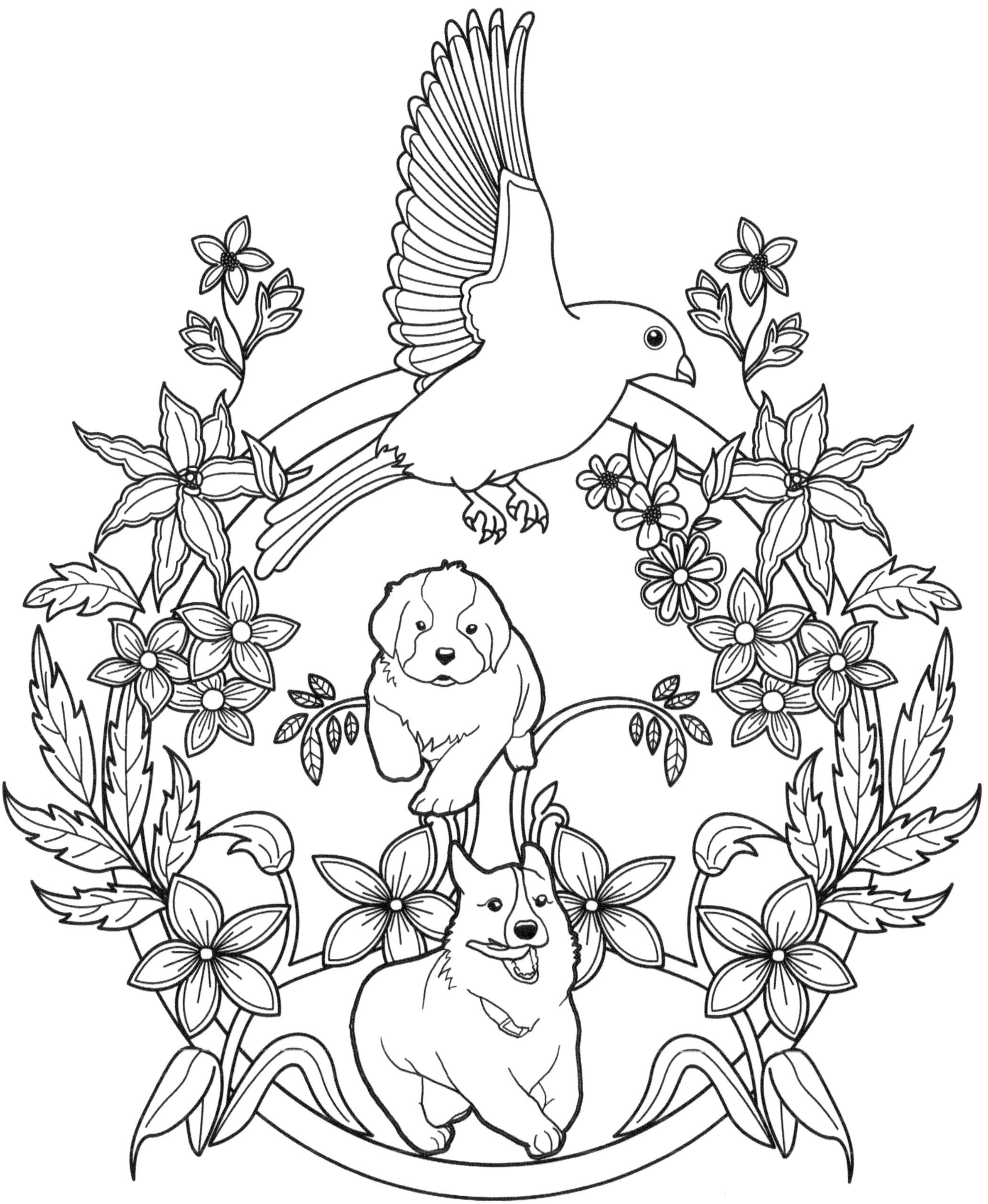

www.ingramcontent.com/pod-product-compliance
Lightning Source LLC
Chambersburg PA
CBHW080640190526
45169CB00009B/3438